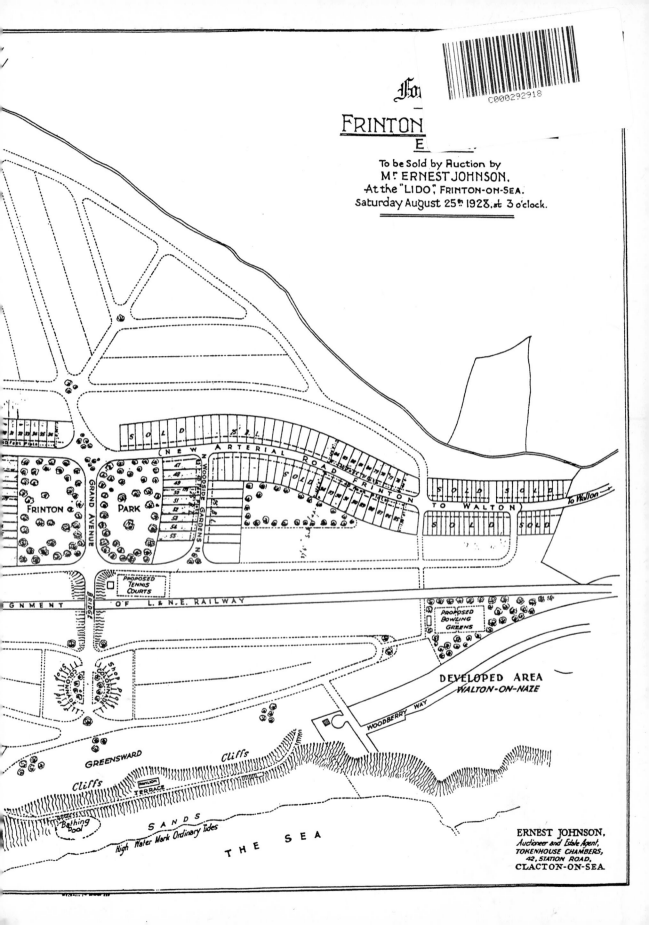

FRINTON
E

To be Sold by Auction by
Mr ERNEST JOHNSON.
At the "LIDO", FRINTON-ON-SEA.
Saturday August 25th 1928, at 3 o'clock.

FRINTON
PARK

GRAND AVENUE

SOLD

NEW ARTERIAL ROAD FRINTON

WOODSIDE GARDENS

SOLD

To WALTON

To Walton

SOLD SOLD

SOLD SOLD SOLD

PROPOSED TENNIS COURTS

ALIGNMENT OF L & N.E. RAILWAY

BRIDGE

PROPOSED BOWLING GREENS

DEVELOPED AREA
WALTON-ON-NAZE

WOODBERRY WAY

GREENSWARD

Cliffs

Cliffs

PAVILION
TERRACE

Bathing Pool

SANDS
High Water Mark Ordinary Tides

THE SEA

ERNEST JOHNSON,
Auctioneer and Estate Agent,
TOKENHOUSE CHAMBERS,
42, STATION ROAD,
CLACTON-ON-SEA

FRINTON & WALTON

A Pictorial History

Frinton-on-Sea.

Particulars, with Plan and Conditions of Sale

OF

100 -MOST ELIGIBLE PLOTS OF

Freehold Building Land,

8 SEASIDE RESIDENCES

AND

2 FREEHOLD SHOPS,

TO BE OFFERED AT AUCTION, BY

MR. EDWIN J. GILDERS,

IN CONJUNCTION WITH

MR. JOHN H. HARMAN,

In the Grounds of the Esplanade Hotel,
On SATURDAY, 15th August, 1903,
At 3 o'clock precisely.

Particulars, Plan, and Conditions of Sale may be had of Messrs. CHAMBERLAYNE & ELWES, Solicitors, Clacton-on-Sea and Frinton-on-Sea ; Messrs. CHAMBERLAYNE & SHELTON, Solicitors, 9 Gracechurch Street, E.C. ; Messrs. CRIDLAND & NELL, Solicitors, 27 Bedford Row, London, W.C. ; Mr. R. W. REGGE, 14 Finsbury Circus, E.C. ; Messrs. HARRINGTON, LEY & TOMLINS, Frinton-on-Sea and 65 Bishopsgate Street, Without, E.C. ; Messrs. HOMER & SHARP, Architects, 11 Old Queen Street, Queen Anne's Gate, S.W. and Frinton-on-Sea ; Mr. WILLIAM HAYNE, Architect, Station Road, Frinton-on-Sea ; at the Grand, Queens, and Esplanade Hotels, and "Beach House", Frinton-on-Sea ; at the "Grand" and "Royal" Hotels, and the "Waverley," Clacton-on-Sea ; and of the Auctioneers :—

MR. EDWIN J. GILDERS, Station Road, Clacton-on-Sea,
And 10 Union Court, Old Broad Street, E.C. ;

MR. JOHN H. HARMAN, Estate Office, Clacton-on-Sea.

The front cover of a 1903 auction catalogue, extolling the virtues of a peaceful life at Frinton-on-Sea.

FRINTON & WALTON
A Pictorial History

Norman Jacobs

Phillimore

1995

Published by
PHILLIMORE & CO. LTD.
Shopwyke Manor Barn, Chichester, West Sussex

ISBN 0 85033 982 0

Printed and bound in Great Britain by
BIDDLES LTD.
Guildford, Surrey

List of Illustrations

Frontispiece: From Rush to Repose

Illustration Acknowledgements

The illustrations appear by kind permission of the following:

Mr. F. Barber, endpapers, frontispiece, 1; Mr. K. Brown, 2, 11, 44, 53, 54, 56, 57, 61, 63, 64, 66, 85, 93, 100, 135, 142; Mrs. J. Burgoyne, 62, 67, 90, 91, 146, 154, 156, 167, 170; Mrs. S. Byatt, 13, 17; Clacton & District Local History Society, 87; Mr. R. Cooper, 6, 7, 16, 68, 70, 92, 94, 96, 105, 131, 148, 152; Mrs. J. Davis, 40; Frinton Golf Club, 121, 122; Frinton-on-Sea Lawn Tennis Club, 124, 125; Mrs. J. Hammond, 60, 65, 69, 83, 84, 89, 158, 168, 169; Mr. W. Harvey, 129, 130; Mr. H. Hatcher, 98, 132; Mr. I. Jay, 3, 4, 15, 18; Mr. D. Johnson, 171; Miss O. Jones, 48-52, 55, 59, 133, 134, 143, 155; Mr. R. Kennell, 32, 41, 111, 116; Kirby Playing Fields Association, 128; Mr. R. Oxley, 145; Mr. P. Pollendine, 75, 76; Putman's Photographers, 30, 35, 39, 45, 77-81, 106, 107, 127, 138-40, 150, 151, 163-6; Mr. M. Rodwell, 5, 12, 58, 97, 99, 110, 141, 160, 161; Mr. G. Taylor, 71-3; Walton Town Football Club, 126, 153. All other illustrations are from the author's own collection.

Acknowledgements

As well as lending me photographs and other illustrations, many of those mentioned above also spent many hours with me reminiscing about old times; to all of them I am very grateful. I would like to say a special thank you, however, to Robin Cooper and Mick Rodwell, whose kindness and patience with me went well above the call of duty! I should also like to thank the Frinton and Walton Heritage Trust, in particular their archivist, Jean Sanderson, for the unflagging help and co-operation so willingly given. Others who have given me time and support include Peter Frost of Putman's Photographers (who not only helped with the supply and copying of photographs, but also filled me in on much of Walton's recent history), Michael Max, Derek Cleaver, Ric Holt, Dora Rose, Urban Wildney, Reg Young, Lt. Col. R.W. Atrill, secretary of Frinton Golf Club and Station Officer Batten of the Frinton fire brigade. I would also like to express my thanks to Barbara Winter, Lisa Bliss and Peter Palmer for their help with the photography. And finally, although I have never met him, I should like to thank Dr. Peter Boyden, whose pioneering work with the Walton-on-the-Naze Records Office and his continuing research and publications in the field of local history have proved such an inspiration.

Introduction

Frinton and Walton – Early History

Frinton-on-Sea and Walton-on-the-Naze are neighbouring seaside resorts lying on the north-east coast of Essex about eighty miles from London. They are both built on London clay which becomes naturally exposed in the cliffs, where it is characterised by nodules of argillaceous limestone, otherwise known as cement-stones or septaria. It is probable that the Romans collected this material from the cliffs in an area stretching from Clacton to Harwich, including Frinton and Walton, for the manufacture of their cement.

At the north-east end of this stretch of coastline, at the Naze itself, is an area of Red Crag, a red-brown sand, which has become famous for its fossil finds, particularly corals, barnacles, molluscs and other shell types. Many of those found are from either extinct species or forms now found in Southern Europe. Few mammal finds have been discovered in this area, but further to the south west, in the Pleistocene deposits, animal remains such as the Celtic shorthorn, spotted hyena, bison, woolly rhinoceros, mammoth and straight-tusked elephant have been found.

It seems probable that early man settled in the area around the Naze, as some Palaeolithic (old stone age) tools have been discovered. What is definite is that Neolithic (new stone age) man (*c.*3500-*c.*2000 B.C.) had an extensive settlement in the area as large numbers of tools, chips and waste have been found and, while the evidence almost certainly points to there having been a flint tool-making factory in the area, the type of material used in a number of the tools shows that some at least were imported from Cornwall, thus pointing also to a sophisticated trading settlement with extensive links to the outside world.

Apart from the use of septaria there is little evidence of Roman occupation in the area, although some Romano-British potsherds were seen in the cliffs at Frinton during building works in the early years of this century.

It is from Saxon times that the present towns of Frinton and Walton can trace their direct lineage and, although by the 20th century both had developed from small rural communities into busy and well-known seaside resorts, the route taken by them was quite different as was the type of resort they became. Even today, although often linked together, they each retain their own separate and distinctive traditions and character.

Frinton

Although the name Frinton is of Saxon origin (from Fritha's tun meaning Fritha's farm), little is known of the village from this period. It is not until Domesday Book in 1086 that anything is heard of it, when it consisted of two manors, confusingly called Frietuna and Frientuna, and appears to have relied on arable farming for its livelihood.

Domesday Book shows that Frinton consisted of something like 12 families and that the male peasant population had been halved from 18 to 9 in 20 years. Frinton was a tiny village, even by 11th-century standards and, over the years, was to grow even smaller.

The decrease in size may have been due to the constant battle Frinton was engaged in against erosion. For example, the chancel of St Mary's, Frinton's Norman church, was destroyed by a severe storm in 1703 while between 1857 and 1865 the churchwarden, Richard Stone, noted: 'The sea is encroaching very fast and it would not surprise me if it [the church] has to be moved back before many years' (1857), 'The parish is gradually wasting' (1862) and 'The sea is still encroaching' (1865). In 1863 St Mary's was approximately 300 yards from the cliff; it is now about half that distance.

The small size and consequent poverty of the village was reflected in a visit to the parish church by Jonas Warley from the archdeaconry of Colchester during his tour of churches between 1705 and 1707. His report on St Mary's makes very depressing reading:

> There is not a decent Communion Table, nor any of the Ornaments nor utensils, viz. Noe carpett, noe table cloth of linnen nor napkin, noe chalice, noe patten. There is noe Bible, noe Common Prayer booke, noe booke of homilies, nor cannon, noe table of marriages, noe Pulpit Cushion, noe Surplice, noe Register booke, noe bell.

Richard Stone also recorded in 1857 that there had been 'no register of birth, marriage or death for many years … our congregation is literally "two or three gathered" … and seldom numbers six'.

This was the situation then in 1885, when the Marine and General Land Company bought up Frinton and, in 1886, published its plans for a town of 'Broad terraces, squares, crescents, tree-lined avenues and roads'. In 1888 a new railway station was built (the line to Walton already ran through Frinton, but it was served only by an unofficial wayside halt) and everything seemed ready for the conversion of Frinton into a bustling seaside town.

And yet, for a few years, very little happened. The population of Frinton had been 55 in 1881. By 1891, that number had risen to just eighty-seven. It was not until Richard Powell-Cooper took a hand by taking over the Development Company and stamping his own ideas and energy on the company that anything really started to happen.

His first big success was building the golf course at the very western end of the parish, bordering on Great Holland, in 1895. The *Grand Hotel* followed in 1898, the Lawn Tennis Club in 1900 and, starting about 1901, Station Road, later to become

Connaught Avenue, was transformed into a high-class shopping street known as 'The Bond Street of East Anglia'.

Richard Powell-Cooper, and later the Frinton Urban District Council, had very definite ideas about the sort of resort they wanted Frinton to become. They definitely did not want it to become like Clacton-on-Sea, the other new resort just along the coast, with its hoards of day trippers, concert parties on the beach, donkey rides, shellfish stalls and all the other paraphernalia of the common seaside resort. Their plan was for a high-class select resort where those who wished it could find peace and tranquillity away from the 'madding crowd'. To this day there are no pubs inside the gates at Frinton.

To combat the age-old problem of coastal erosion, the Frinton Sea Defences Act of 1903 allowed for the building of nearly a mile of concrete sea wall with promenade and groynes. It was as part of this work that Frinton's famous greensward was laid out. By 1911, Frinton's population had risen to just over one and a half thousand.

Frinton's halcyon days were probably the years between the wars, when for part of the summer season the town became the social centre for anyone who was anyone. The annual lawn tennis tournament and the golf club attracted names such as the Prince of Wales, Winston Churchill, Gladys Cooper, Gracie Fields, Douglas Fairbanks and many other leading socialites of the day, who would rent houses for weeks at a time in the Avenues and other select roads in Frinton.

It was during this period, the 1920s and '30s, that a grand new extension was envisaged for Frinton, known as the Frinton Park Estate. It was an area to the east of the town and was planned to connect Frinton to Walton. The endpapers of this book show its proposed location and also the proposed size of the development. Part of the plan was to move the railway line further inland away from the cliffs (once again due to fears from erosion). This was carried out in 1930 and the old trackbed used as the foundation of Waltham Way.

After several portions of the estate had been sold off to individual developers, the rest was bought by the South Coast Property Investment Company Ltd. in 1934 and was handed over to a management company called Frinton Park Estate Ltd. Oliver Hill, their consultant architect, drew up a detailed scheme which included new roads, a college, churches and a 100-room luxury hotel facing the sea. The architecture of the new houses and other buildings was to be carried out in the most up-to-date art deco manner; and, to show he meant business, Oliver Hill designed the Estate Office itself as a circular building with curving interior walls and a mosaic floor laid out as a plan of the estate.

It proved itself to be too modern for Frinton and buyers stayed away. Within little more than a year the plan was abandoned and, although some houses were built and can still be seen, including the Round House (Estate Office), the land was eventually covered with more conventional buildings, while the college, churches and luxury hotel remained just a concept in the planner's mind.

When the Second World War came, Frinton was evacuated as it formed part of the 'coastal strip', which was taken over by the army. Anyone not having business in the town was asked to leave. Naval guns were sited below the *Grand Hotel* and the cliffs there reinforced with iron girders, which are still in place today and still protect that part of the coastline from Frinton's old enemy—erosion. Some bomb damage was experienced in Frinton, including much damage at Ratcliffe's Garage and the Service Garage in Connaught Avenue.

With the return of peace in 1946, Frinton once again took up its position as a select seaside resort. However, in common with most seaside resorts in the country, and especially in Essex, it was never to be quite as popular as it had been before the war. It was no longer the social centre for celebrities that it had once been and, when lawn tennis went 'open' in the late 1960s, the big names stopped coming. Its final fling was probably the ladies final of 1970, when the current Wimbledon singles champion, Margaret Court, defeated the 1969 champion, Ann Jones, in a thrilling match.

Gradually most of the big hotels closed and were either knocked down or became retirement homes. Only the *Maplin* and the *Rock*, of any size, are open today.

Like most other resorts in this part of Essex, Frinton's appeal today is to the day tripper rather than the long-stay visitor. The resident population, however, continues to grow, both inside and outside the gates, as many people seek a peaceful retirement and commuters seek the charms of the seaside as a release from their work in the City.

Walton-on-the-Naze

A number of explanations have been put forward for the origin of the name Walton, ranging from Wall Town to the equally spurious Whale Town, called after a beached whale! Although it is still not absolutely certain, the most likely explanation is that the name Walton derives from the Saxon words *weala tun*, meaning farms of Britons. If this is correct it raises the interesting point that when the Saxons arrived they must have found a thriving Romano-British community in the area.

The other part of the name, on-the-Naze, is also somewhat problematic and again it is necessary to guess rather than to state with any absolute certainty. But the most likely origin for this is *Aelduluesnasa*, or *Aedwulfsness*, meaning Edwulf's Promontory, though who Edwulf might have been is another matter.

At one time, the name Aelduluesnasa was applied to the whole area, including the three Soken parishes of Thorpe-le-Soken, Kirby-le-Soken and Walton, which used to be known as Walton-le-Soken. In her book *Aelduluesnasa: Kirby in History*, Rosemary Pratt conjectures that Aelduluesnasa became shortened in time, through various well established linguistic conventions, to Altun's Naze, thus obviating the need to seek any explanation for the Walton part of the name.

As stated above, the origin of the name Walton-on-the-Naze has still not definitely been determined. What has been determined, however, is that Walton, along with Thorpe and Kirby, formed a separate unit of legal jurisdiction known as the Sokens. Although most of Essex had fallen under the see of London from as early as the seventh century, the Sokens had always formed part of the peculiars of the chapter of St Paul's, with certain rights, duties and privileges granted to all those living in the area. These included property rights, differences in the way land was held, duties owed to the lord of the manor and separate courts. Domesday Book shows Aelduluesnasa to have consisted of 40 smallholders, 86 villagers and six slaves.

Like Frinton, Walton's history has also been dominated by its fight against erosion. In the Middle Ages, the whole town seems to have been situated in what is now the North Sea. Certainly the original medieval church was lost to the waves in the latter part of the 18th century and early years of the nineteenth.

Daniel Defoe, in his *A Tour Through the Whole Island of Great Britain*, written in 1724, reported that in 'Walton under the Nase … the sea gains so much upon the land here … that within the memory of some of the inhabitants there, they have lost above 30 acres of land in one place'.

Yet further evidence of the location of the original Walton and its loss to coastal erosion comes in Thomas Wilmshurst's *Descriptive Account of Walton-on-the-Naze*, published in 1860. This includes some reminiscences from a 'cheerful, garrulous old lady … verging on ninety years'. She told Wilmshurst that she could remember 'a field, two cottages, and a public house—the *Duke's Head*' which, she said, were actually to the seaward side of the old church.

Although Walton was a largely agricultural village, there is some evidence of maritime activity as, for example, in 1342, when Walton supplied one ship for King Edward III's expedition to Brittany and then in 1572 when Thomas Colshill, surveyor of customs at London, noted that Walton had one ship in the '20 tons and under' category.

But it was the manufacture of copperas into green copperas or green vitriol that at one time almost rivalled the farming interest of Walton. Copperas stones (bisulphide of iron), made from the pyritous nodules of clay found in cliffs, were washed out by the action of the waves and gathered from the beach by women and children to be taken to the copperas houses for manufacture. In 1696 there were two copperas houses situated just to the west of the High Street, near where the library is today. Early on, in the 13th century, green copperas was used for sheep-dressing, but by the 18th century it was used for dyeing, tanning and the manufacture of ink.

The industry's eventual decline in the early 19th century coincided with the decline of the wool and tanning industries in East Anglia, although some copperas was still being gathered in 1880 to be sent to Ipswich for use in the manufacture of sulphuric acid.

As late as 1907, it was noted in the *Victoria County History of Essex* that the space where the copperas works had been was 'still bare of vegetation and so saturated with sulphurous matter that … the floors of the few houses built on the edge of this ground, quickly became corroded'.

It is impossible to say when the first holiday visitor arrived at Walton, having been attracted by its sandy beach or enticed by its sea bathing potential. As early as 1772, John Crosier of Maldon was known to have visited Walton, and in 1805, John Hanson, Deputy Lieutenant of Tendring, took part in picnic parties on Walton beach.

By 1818, John Aldridge was advertising his *Bath House Hotel* and, shortly afterwards, his bathing machines. But it was in 1829 that two events happened that were really to mark the beginning of Walton-on-the-Naze as a seaside resort.

The first was the publication of the first guide to Walton. The other was the opening of *The Hotel*, later *The Marine Hotel*, which over the years seemed to acquire the habit of either officially or unofficially naming itself after its owner; hence it was later known as *Dorling's, Kent's* and *Barker's*!

The Hotel had 24 sitting rooms and bedrooms, a coffee lounge and a ballroom. It attracted trade away from the *Bath House*, which resulted in the centre of Walton itself shifting slightly to the area around *The Hotel*, with further streets being built in its vicinity.

In 1830 another major event in Walton's progress to a major seaside resort took place when a small pier was built directly in front of *The Hotel*. Although only 150 ft. in length, it was intended as a landing stage for Ipswich and London steam ships, but even after it was lengthened to 330 ft. in 1848 it was still not enough to take steamers at low tide.

It should also be mentioned that there was one other hotel in Walton at this time, the *Portobello Hotel* in the High Street, which seems to have been rebuilt around this period.

It was in this vicinity then that Walton's growth began and new houses were built in the streets around this centre, in Old Pier Street, High Street, Saville Street and Newgate Street. In 1821 the population of Walton had stood at 293, by 1831 it had risen to 469, and by 1841 it was to rise still further to 721. By then, however, a further development had taken place and with it an attempt to shift the centre of Walton to the east.

In 1834 John Warner, a bellfounder from Hoddesdon, Hertfordshire, bought an area of land further up the coast and proceeded to build a terrace of seven houses, together with a reading room and bazaar and two cottages. In total Warner bought up a large area of land stretching from the backwaters to the road out to Kirby, but he never developed most of it and so his scheme, in the end, did not really detract from the centre of Walton, which remained firmly where it was.

Warner's terrace, known as East Terrace, included one house at the near end larger and grander than the rest, with a fine porch, which he kept for his own use. This later became the *Eastcliff Hotel* and is today the *Naze Mariner*.

In 1840 another guide to Walton was published, called *An Historical and Geographical Description of the Favourite Watering Place of Walton-on-the-Naze*. This mentions the regatta, probably Walton's first major laid-on holiday entertainment, which had begun about 1830 and attracted large numbers of visitors to Walton every summer to take part in the sailing and rowing races and other events. Or, as the guide put it, 'A great number of persons of all classes from the surrounding parishes and some from a great distance honour it with their presence'. It also went on to say that: 'A band of music is stationed near the *Hotel* which gives *éclat* to the scene'.

1855 saw the arrival of civil engineer Peter Bruff on the Walton scene when he bought Burnt House Farm and all the land attached to it. Bruff put a tremendous amount of energy into building up his part of Walton and, thanks largely to him, Walton's fortunes, which had been in the doldrums, revived a little. In 1859 he built the row of houses known as Marine Terrace, followed soon after by South Crescent (or South Terrace). He then set about improving the water supply and the gas supply by sinking an artesian well and building a gas works.

In 1862 he opened the Clifton Baths, also known as the Clifton Music Hall, which included a 350-seat theatre as well as a reading room, a billiards room and indoor baths. It was later renamed the *Clifton Hotel* and, later still, the *Pier Hotel*.

Bruff then started work, in 1869, on a new pier opposite his hotel. Although he had envisaged a much longer pier it was, by 1880, still only 600 ft. in length and in stiff competition with Walton's first pier. However, in January 1881 a heavy storm destroyed the old pier, leaving only the new pier and with it Bruff in sole charge of Walton's steam ship trade.

It was also Bruff who was responsible for bringing the railway to Walton. He had been the engineer on the original Eastern Counties line from London to Colchester, and then, in 1864, he started work on the Tendring hundred line extension to Walton-on-the-Naze. The railway finally arrived on 17 May 1867 at a station built, not surprisingly, at the south end of the resort, near to the *Clifton Hotel* and Bruff's other developments.

In 1878, Bruff attempted a much further-reaching development for the town and, indeed, for Frinton as well, when he proposed a marine drive, promenade and roadway from Walton along the coast as far as Pole Barn Lane, the boundary with Frinton. He also proposed a road to run from Frinton church to the Battery House, near the Great Holland boundary, as well as landscaping the cliffs and making them accessible. In addition he proposed a tramway to run from Walton all the way to the Battery House with spurs to Walton station and the Frinton level crossing.

The bill proposing these measures received Royal Assent on 21 July 1879 but, unfortunately, due to the costs involved, Bruff was never able to start work on this grand scheme and Frinton and Walton had to wait a long time before they eventually became joined in the way envisaged. The tramway was, of course, never built.

By 1880 Bruff had other plans, mainly at his new town of Clacton-on-Sea and at Coalport, where he bought the china factory and, although he still took an interest in Walton, his days of active participation in the town were over.

Bruff's development to the south, then, was another attempt to shift the town centre and, although the *Clifton Hotel* and the pier certainly played a bigger part in the life of Walton than the Eastcliff development, they still did not really alter the main High Street, Old Pier Street, Newgate Street axis at the centre.

One final attempt was made to move the centre of Walton when, in the 1880s, Philip Brannon planned his development at Naze Park. But this development was much too far out of the centre to attract many holidaymakers or even residents and all that he managed to achieve in the end was Naze Park Road itself and a certain amount of coast protection works at the Naze undercliff (Hipkin's Beach).

In 1897 Bruff sold his remaining interests in the town, the pier and the *Clifton Hotel*, to the Walton-on-the-Naze Hotel and Pier Company. In 1899 the company went bankrupt and was taken over by the Coast Development Company (later Corporation), who were also responsible for Clacton's pier and the Belle Steamers. They set about improving the pier, not only to make it more accessible to steamers, by lengthening it to a distance of 2,610 ft., but also by taking the first steps towards turning it into an entertainment centre by building a 750-seat pavilion for shows and concerts, refreshment rooms, a shooting saloon, the headquarters of the Walton swimming club and, perhaps most ambitious of all, an electric railway running the length of the pier.

As Walton continued to grow as a popular seaside resort, other attractions began to spring up around the town in the late 19th and early 20th centuries. There was the Camera Obscura on Albion Beach, the bathing machines, operated by Charles Bates, and later Mary Bates and Stephen Carter. There was sailing to be enjoyed on the Backwaters and pleasure boats operating from the Mill Pond round to the pier. The Regatta continued to attract large numbers, both as participants and as spectators.

In 1900 the new town hall was built in the High Street, including a 700-seat theatre, the King's Theatre. There was a concert party stand at Albion Beach, and later one near the Round Gardens, where refreshments were also available. Walton's population in 1901 stood at 2,014.

Walton's popularity continued to grow after the First World War, with thousands upon thousands of visitors arriving every week. Some returned year after year to their regular booking in 'Hut Town', many came down on spec and would often just tap on any door around Walton and ask, 'Can you take us in for board and lodging for the week?' Very often the answer would be yes!

In the early '20s there were still four shows available to the holidaymaker, though the open-air ones soon packed up, leaving just the pier pavilion and the King's Theatre.

The cinema also came to Walton, first with the opening of the Kino on Princes Esplanade, and then, in 1934, with the much more luxurious Regal opening in the High Street; its first public performance being *Every Woman's Man*, starring Myrna Loy and William Powell, on 7 May.

After the old tide mill was demolished in 1921, the mill pond was turned into a boating lake, open till at least 8.00 at night, while the area occupied by the windmill, also demolished in 1921, was taken over by the Walton Yacht Club.

Towards the end of the 1930s, the pier was bought by the Goss family and, because the paddle steamer trade was now being rapidly replaced by the train, the charabanc and the private car, they decided the future for the pier lay in amusements and so they set about building rides and other forms of entertainment, though much of this work was cut short by the Second World War.

One final major scheme that took place in the '20s was the opening of the Naze Golf Links in 1928; its proud boast was that there was 'a view of the North Sea from every hole'.

As with Frinton, the Second World War put an end to practically all holiday activity in Walton as the town emptied. Walton also suffered some bomb damage, most notably to Bruff's South Terrace, which was completely destroyed.

Walton celebrated the end of the war by burning effigies of German leaders on the Naze and then set about picking up the pieces of its broken holiday trade. The pier, which had been partially destroyed during the war to prevent an enemy landing, was quickly back into action. Rebuilt, a number of new rides were added, including a large ferris wheel and the dodgems. Later on a bowling alley was built which proved to be very popular and led to Walton Pier becoming one of the best ten-pin bowling teams in the country.

Again like Frinton, Walton was to find that things had changed in the post-war years and holidaymakers no longer returned in the same numbers. Live theatrical shows disappeared and, by the late 1960s, both cinemas had closed as well.

Although a recent revival of entertainment facilities has taken place with the building of a small leisure centre on the Bath House Meadow, including a swimming pool and an indoor bowling green and the Columbine Centre, it has done nothing to prevent the trend moving away from the residential holiday. By the 1980s practically all of Walton's big hotels had closed, only the *Pier Hotel* remaining open. Such long-stay holidaymakers as there are now tend to use the caravan parks–the Martello Caravan Park and the Naze Marine Holiday Park.

Walton still has its fine sandy beaches and its shops selling candy floss, sticks of rock and seaside postcards. It still has its pier and its amusement arcades. It still attracts the summer day visitor and the yachting enthusiast but, in the main, it has settled down to being chiefly a residential town for the commuter and for retired people looking for their ideal home by the sea.

Kirby and Great Holland

It would not really be possible to produce a book on Frinton and Walton without including the neighbouring villages of Kirby and Great Holland. Geographically, the four sit together forming a triangular piece of land bounded by the North Sea to the east, Hamford Water to the north and Holland Brook to the south, on the Naze portion of the Tendring peninsula. Three of them (Great Holland, Frinton and Walton) share a common coastline, while to the north, the backwaters link Walton and Kirby.

Ecclesiastically, Walton and Kirby were very much linked as peculiars of the living of St Paul's while the unique legal position of Walton and Kirby in the Sokens has already been outlined.

Historically and politically too, the four parishes have been very much interlinked. A fact which was recognised when the four were combined to form the Frinton and Walton Urban District Council. Even today, after absorption into Tendring District Council in the early '70s, the Frinton and Walton Town Council still operates as the lowest tier of local government for the four parishes.

Although such an integral part of the whole, Kirby and Great Holland do, nevertheless, have their own history and their own traditions. Strange as it may seem now, for many years they were the two largest villages of the four. The first modern census, taken in 1801, showed the following populations: Kirby, 664; Great Holland, 300; Walton, 221 and Frinton, 31. It was not until the 1871 census that Walton finally overtook Kirby as the largest village.

Neither, however, got caught up in the seaside holiday mania that swept the country in the 19th century and both have remained comparatively small and compact, albeit in Kirby's case around two centres, Kirby Cross (Upper Kirby) and Kirby-le-Soken (Lower Kirby), with both retaining a village atmosphere.

One change that has occurred is the loss of shops and businesses as people tend to migrate to the local shopping centres and supermarkets in and around Clacton and Colchester. At one time, for example, Great Holland boasted a number of shops, including a bakery, a general store, a bicycle repairer, a post office, a hat shop, an antiques shop and a dairy, as well as the famous Ratcliffe's Foundry. Now the village is down to one general store on the Clacton road. It is a similar story in Kirby, although it has managed to maintain slightly more of its shops, especially in Upper Kirby.

The whole area has been lucky over the years in having a number of high quality photographers ready and able to record the local scene, local events and local people. From Thomas Dunningham (a surgeon-turned-photographer), who began taking photographs of Walton as early as 1859, through George Woodard of Thorpe-le-Soken in the early years of this century, to Frank Putman, who started in 1921 and whose studio continues to this day still recording the life of the area.

The photographs in this book will bring back memories of the changing times experienced by the people of all four communities, whether that experience is of a small rural community, a close-knit town community or a bustling holiday resort, and will recreate for newcomers the life and spirit of those times gone by.

Frinton-on-Sea

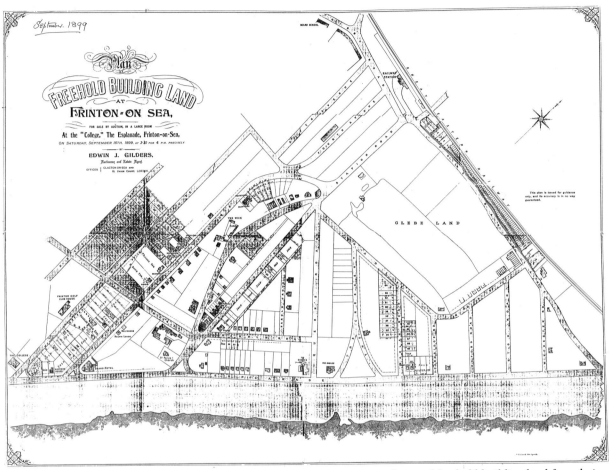

1 A map of Frinton in 1899. This was used to accompany an auction catalogue of freehold building land for sale in the new town of Frinton-on-Sea. The resort was then barely ten years old.

2 The view into Frinton across the famous level crossing gates taken just after the Second World War at a time when the gas supply was still provided by the Tendring Hundred Waterworks Company.

3 A pre-1904 view of Connaught Avenue, in the days when it was merely called Station Road.

4   A later Edwardian view of Connaught Avenue. The high-class shops built along Connaught Avenue during this period earned it the soubriquet of the 'Bond Street of East Anglia'.

5   This postcard of Connaught Avenue was posted in 1919, though the view probably just pre-dates the First World War. On the right is Oliver Parker & Co., grocers. They arrived in Connaught Avenue about 1910 and remained until the late 1960s. At one time Oliver Parker had the sole concession for Tiptree jam in Frinton, much to the annoyance of the other grocery shops!

6   A late 1920s view of Connaught Avenue showing Mummery's House Furnishing shop. Mummery (later Mummery & Harris) had two shops in Connaught Avenue, one on each side of the road. The one in the photograph is where the Midland Bank is today. The one on the other side of the road was destroyed by fire in 1936 (see plate 147).

7 A view of the other side of Connaught Avenue from about the same period showing Blowers & Cooper's hardware shop. Blowers & Cooper first set up business in Frinton in 1903 at 7 Old Road, moving to Connaught Avenue in 1910. The shop is still there today under the management of Robin Cooper, grandson of one of the original partners.

8 An unusual view of Connaught Avenue dating from about the time of the First World War. It is looking north towards the station before that part of the avenue was built up.

Connaught Avenue & Free Church, Frinton-on-Sea.

9   The Free Church on the right at the bottom of Connaught Avenue was built in 1912. Interestingly, this postcard was sent by a soldier stationed in Frinton during the First World War. His message on the back reads: 'The school of church at right is our mess room. Corner shop opposite is Qtr. Master Stores'.

10   In 1935 a tower was added to the Free Church as can be seen in this photograph taken in the late 1940s.

11   An old print of St Mary's Church, said to be one of the smallest churches in England. Parts of the nave date back to Norman times, but the chancel was completely rebuilt in 1879 having lain in ruins for over 170 years.

12   As a memorial to those who died in the First World War, a gun was placed in the gardens at the junction of Connaught Avenue and Old Road in 1920. It was cut up with an acetylene cutter and removed for scrap in 1940. While this was being done, the boys who crowded round to watch were greatly amused when the workman cutting up the gun fell off it into a cactus bush nearby!

13 Pole Barn Lane was a source of great controversy between Frinton and Walton in the early years of this century. The boundary between the two ran down the middle of the road, but Frinton claimed it would be better served if they owned all of it. Following a local government enquiry, and despite Walton's objections, Frinton was 'awarded' Pole Barn Lane in September 1904.

14 Frinton's Greensward, *c.*1912, in the days when the grass was kept short by allowing sheep to graze on it. It is, however, a complete myth that there was ever a law forbidding picnicking there.

15 Frinton's development in the late 19th century centred mainly on the area near the golf course in Second, Third and Fourth Avenues. It was also this part of Frinton that played host to the celebrities that visited Frinton in the '20s and '30s.

16 The Esplanade in the early years of this century. On the left can just be seen the drinking fountain built to celebrate Edward VII's coronation in 1902. On the right is the *Esplanade Hotel.*

11 FRINTON-ON-SEA. — *Esplanade Hotel* — LL.

17 The *Esplanade Hotel* was built in 1902, and this photograph dates from just two or three years later. The *Esplanade* was one of a number of hotels built around that time to cater for the growing holiday trade. Others included *The Queens*, *The Grand*, *The Rock* and *The Maplin*. The *Esplanade* later became *Hildenborough Hall*.

18 In the days before the present Walton Road was built, the main route from Frinton to Walton was straight across the level crossing and along Elm Tree Avenue, then known as Walton Road. This is a view looking along that Walton Road towards the level crossing in the early years of this century.

19 Mr. Bright, the last level crossing keeper to live in the gate keeper's cottage, closes the gates on Frinton. He retired in 1959. The cottage is now the headquarters of the Frinton and Walton Heritage Trust.

Walton-on-the-Naze

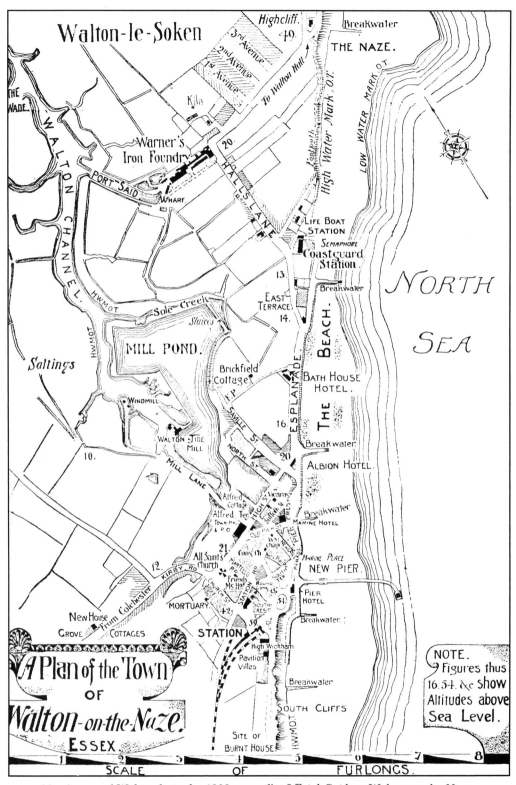

20 A map of Walton from the 1908 council's *Official Guide* to Walton-on-the-Naze.

21 A very early view of Walton-on-the-Naze taken from an engraving drawn for *The History and Topography of the County of Essex* by Thomas Wright, published in 1836. On the extreme left is the *Marine Hotel*, built in 1829 and leading out from that Walton's original pier, built in 1830.

22 An early view of the *Marine Hotel*, originally called simply *The Hotel* and later *Dorling's*, from the old pier. It was around this hotel that the seaside resort of Walton-on-the-Naze sprang up in the 1830s.

23   In 1836, John Warner, who originally came from Hertfordshire, tried to move the centre of Walton further east by building a new terrace of lodging houses for summer visitors. His own house was at the end of the terrace and included a fine porch and other improvements which the others did not have. Warner's house is now the *Naze Mariner*.

24   In the late 1850s and '60s, Peter Bruff attempted to move the centre of Walton in the other direction and built South Terrace (on the left), Marine Terrace (in the centre) and the Clifton Baths (on the right). This photograph dates from the late 1860s, but before 1869, in which year Bruff started work on his pier.

25 Another photograph taken in the 1860s, this time of Morton Terrace at the corner of Old Pier Street and Newgate Street in the area known as the Six Releat. In spite of the attempts to shift the centre of Walton it remained around its original nucleus, running back from the *Marine Hotel*, up Old Pier Street and into the High Street.

26 West Street, *c.*1890. In the background is Walton's church before the tower was added in 1895/6. On the right is Henry James' baker's shop. Henry James had a baker shop in Walton from about 1870 until about 1910. West Street was incorporated into the High Street in the mid-1890s.

27   The first of four photographs showing the changing face of the High Street. This one was taken prior to 1900 and shows the old thatched cottage known as The Hoy.

28 This one also shows The Hoy, but the open space next to it has been replaced by the Town Hall, built in 1900 at a cost of £8,000. Downstairs was Barclays Bank and the post office.

29 By 1906, The Hoy had disappeared and had been replaced by High Street shops including, as can be seen here, the International Stores.

30 The same view in 1957. The International Stores and Barclays Bank are still there but the council offices have gone. This photograph shows the paraffin lorry delivering supplies to P.C. Phillpott, ironmonger and decorators' supplies. The one constant building in all these photographs is the *Portobello Hotel* on the right-hand side. Probably built in the 1820s on the site of an earlier inn, it lasted as an hotel for something like 160 years.

31 Walton's All Saints' Church in the 1960s. This is on the site of the church built in 1804 to replace the medieval building rendered unusable by coastal erosion at the end of the 18th century. Because Walton was continually growing in size throughout the 19th century, the church was enlarged in the 1830s and then completely rebuilt in the 1870s. The final touch came when the tower was added in 1896.

32 A view of Walton from the church tower just after it was built. Looking along the High Street, the first building on the right is the *Portobello Hotel.*

33 In 1902 this building, Walton Lodge, was built by P.G. Oxley just in front of the *Portobello Hotel*, on the corner of Portobello Road. This site has since been occupied by the Regal cinema and Woolworth's.

34 Further along the High Street in about 1910 was F.A. Collins' baker shop and Haven Puxley's fishmonger's. Mr. Collins was the leader of the Progressive Party on Walton-on-the-Naze Urban District Council during its early years and was the Honorary Secretary of Walton Football Club.

35 Now reaching the end of the High Street, *c.*1950, just past the post office on the left with C. Oldridge's tobacconist on the right and the *Royal Albion Hotel* in the far distance.

36 The *Clifton Hotel* as seen from Peter Bruff's new pier in the 1890s. Built in 1862 it was originally known as Clifton Baths or Clifton Music Hall and contained a small theatre seating around 350.

37 After the Walton Pier and Hotel Company bought the hotel in 1896 its name changed to the *Pier Hotel*. This photograph dates from about 1906.

38 The corner of The Parade and New Pier Street just before the Second World War, with Peter Bruff's South Terrace in the background. South Terrace was completely destroyed in the war. Notice also the advertising board for Woolworth's; not the one in Walton as there was not one at the time! This is for the Woolworth's in Connaught Avenue, Frinton.

39 Old Pier Street in 1957. In the middle distance is the terrace known as Morton Terrace (see plate 25), now converted into shops. On the right is the main entrance to the *Marine Hotel*.

40 The start of Princes Esplanade by Albion Beach. This has always been a busy corner with, in the early years of the 20th century, concert parties and a camera obscura and, by the time of this photograph, *c.*1930, a bus and taxi stand, a refreshment kiosk and the well-loved Hipkin's ice-cream cart.

41 Further along Princes Esplanade towards East Terrace, *c.*1905. On the left, next to the 'Ladies', is the *Bath House Hotel*, probably Walton's first hotel as it seems to have been operational before 1820. Being built right on the sea front it is said that, during high tides, water used to come in the front door and flood out of the back! The hotel was demolished in 1936.

42 The Marine Gardens, originally the green at the foot of Walton's first pier, was the site of Walton's memorial gun. Set up at the same time as Frinton's memorial gun (see plate 12), it suffered the same fate.

43 Development of the Naze Park Estate began in the 1880s by Philip Brannon. Being so far from the centre it was slow going, however. By the time of this photograph, taken in Hall Lane just before the First World War, not much seems to have happened at all!

44 The main house on the estate was Brannon's own and was called Hygeia Lodge (seen in the foreground). It is now Putman's Photographic Studio. This photograph dates from about 1952.

45   The Naze Cliffs in the mid-1950s. In the background is the Naze Tower, built originally in 1720 by Trinity House as a warning signal for ships entering Harwich and enlarged in 1796. This part of the coast has suffered untold damage from erosion over the years and is still a source of constant worry. Even much of the land shown in this photograph from just 40 years ago has now disappeared.

46 Walton's tide mill, *c.*1910. There are records of a watermill on this spot going back until at least 1400. For much of the 19th century the mill was owned by John Archer. The mill was eventually demolished in 1921 and the mill pond turned into a boating lake.

47 Close to the tide mill was the windmill, a post mill, again operated by John Archer in the 19th century. The windmill was also demolished in 1921 and the site became the headquarters of the Yacht Club.

Kirby

48   Heading from Frinton towards Upper Kirby in the 1920s. On the right are Kirby's new shops, while on the left is the Pondtail Filling Station, later to become Coronation Garage.

49 Kirby Cross in the 1930s. On the left the A.A. patrol man discusses the state of the roads with the postman! The cottages on the right were knocked down to allow for road widening.

50 From about the same period, the A.A. man poses outside his telephone box on the island at the junction of Halstead Road and Frinton Road. Behind the box is the 'Coronation Tree' planted in 1911.

51 Station Corner in the late 1920s. On the left is the Bonnet Box, built *c.*1925 and run for many years by Mrs. Annie Young. On the other side of Station Road is the *Station Tavern*, opened in *c.*1880. It is now called the *Kirby Tavern*, but curiously has a picture of a train on its name board.

52 Upper Kirby's grocery and provision shop just before the First World War at about the time it came into the hands of the Page family.

53 At the end of the war, Dick Page got married and had the house on the left built next to his shop. He also turned part of the shop into living accommodation, as can be seen in this photograph from the late 1920s. The shop eventually became Bailey's Stores and stopped trading in the 1970s.

54 Looking in the opposite direction and on the other side of the road, this view of Thorpe Road, Upper Kirby, shows Melbourne Cottage, Melbourne House, 1 and 2 Victory Cottages and, just beyond, the *Hare and Hounds* public house. The date is about 1902.

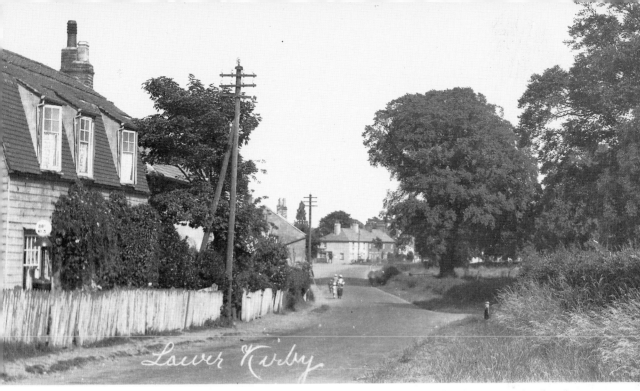

Lower Kirby

55 This is the cottage known as Sunnyside in Lower Kirby, *c.*1930. It was owned by the Bennett family who ran a film distribution service for all the local cinemas. Mr. Urban Wildney, their driver, used to fill up the van from the petrol pump seen here in the garden and drive to London to exchange the week's films.

56 John Wagstaff, grocer and draper, had his shop in Lower Kirby from about 1905 until the late 1920s. The shed adjacent to the shop once housed a steam-powered threshing machine.

57 C.D. Skingley's draper and grocer shop was a feature of The Street from the late 1890s, when it was known as Skingley and Leeds, until the early 1920s, by which time it had also become Kirby-le-Soken's post office. The cottages next to Skingley's were known as Malting Cottages and were originally a maltings.

58 Outside Robert Oxborrow's forge near the corner with Halstead Road in the early years of this century.

59 Lower Street, now known as Walton Road, *c.*1910. The shop in the middle on the right (Brenteleigh) was owned at this time by Sydney H. Garrod. It later became a general store under the ownership of S. Harris. Victoria Avenue and Edith Road can just be made out on the right.

Great Holland

60 *(above)* The ancient *Ship Inn* in the heart of the village. At the time of this photograph, taken *c.*1912, it was owned by Frederick Overton.

61 *(above right)* Looking up Manor Road from the *Ship Inn* towards Main Road. On the left is the post office. When this photograph was taken, *c.*1905, the Village Hall and Institute had not yet been built.

62 *(right)* Great Holland's schoolchildren line up to have their photograph taken at the bottom of Manor Road, *c.*1912. On the left is the post office again, but by now, the Village Hall and Institute beyond had become a feature of the village.

63 The Village Hall and Institute was built in 1909 and used for many village events and exhibitions, such as this one, the Horticultural Exhibition, held in 1911.

64 Originally known as *The Lion*, it became the *Red Lion* at about the time of this photograph, *c.*1910, and later changed its name yet again to become the *Lion's Den*. It is on the corner of Clacton Road and what is now Little Clacton Road, formerly known as Common Road.

65 Henry Ratcliffe, on the left in this photograph, moved from Yorkshire to Great Holland in the late 1880s. His ironworks in Old Manor Road became one of the largest businesses in the area. He lived next door to the foundry in this house, named Hunslet.

66 Woodcot, the one-time home of James Peachey, owner of the village nurseries and donor of the Peachey Quoits Cup, which was played for annually on the lawn at the back of the *Ship*.

67 Great Holland Mill in its days as a working mill. Built originally in 1840 by Mr. James Beckwith to replace an earlier mill, it was struck by lightning in 1858 and considerable damage was done. By 1937 the sails were no longer working and they were locked into position and eventually removed. On Christmas Eve 1986 the stump was destroyed by fire.

Shops and Business

68 Richard Denly and Son, butchers and poulterers of 4 Connaught Avenue, Frinton. The *East Essex Advertiser* of 24 December 1904 reported: 'All that is needed in the way of prime joints for the Christmas table can be obtained from Messrs. R. Denly & Son'. Unfortunately their prime joints were unable to save the business–they had gone from Connaught Avenue by 1912.

69 George Wortley's greengrocery business was also situated in Connaught Avenue and lasted from about 1904 until the First World War. The boy holding the horse is Charlie Clouting, grandson of Mrs. Smith, Frinton's postmistress. The site is now occupied by Bambi.

70 Blowers and Cooper's new shop being built by Ovenden the builders at 28-30 Connaught Avenue in 1912. Both Thomas Blowers and George Cooper had originally come from Diss in Norfolk. Thomas Blowers retired in 1928, but George Cooper continued working until 1962, finally retiring in his 92nd year!

71 *(above)*   William Taylor opened his grocer's shop at 23 Connaught Avenue in 1902, having arrived in Frinton from Wandsworth Bridge Road, London.

72 *(top right)*   He hoped to buy premises on the opposite side of Connaught Avenue for use as an off-licence, but owing to objections from the church he was forced to give up the idea. Instead he bought the shop next door (no.21) and turned that into a licensed grocer's.

73 *(bottom right)*   By the 1920s William Taylor had merged the two shops into one unit. The business was eventually taken over by his son, Percy William and then by this grandson, Graham. It lasted until the 1970s.

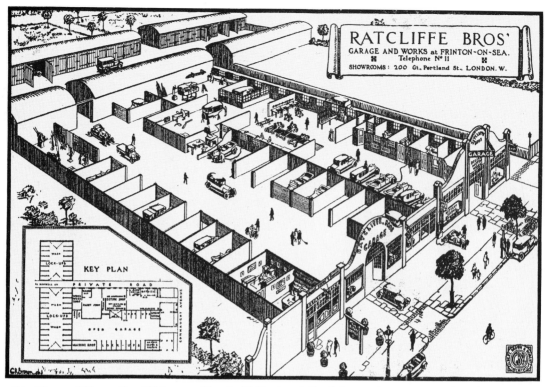

74 Three of Henry Ratcliffe's sons, Claude, Telford and Cyril, began their motor and cycle works in Frinton's Connaught Avenue in 1900. The other brother, Archie, stayed with his father for many years at Great Holland until he too moved to Frinton to open his gardening shop. It was Archie's son-in-law, Ted Hammond, who eventually took over the Ratcliffes' motor works and founded Hammond Motors.

75 The Service Garage, also in Connaught Avenue, pictured in the late 1920s. Leo Stanley, on the right of the group, worked for the garage all his life, eventually becoming its manager.

76 The Service Garage was badly damaged by a bomb during the Second World War and was rebuilt in the late 1940s. In 1968, the date of this photograph, the garage was bought by Peter Pollendine and his wife Rita and renamed Pollendine's in 1970.

77 Roy Putman, the manager, and Mrs. James (standing in the shop doorway) organise the newsboys' and girls' annual outing from their shop Mark James & Son at 63 High Street, Walton, in September 1953. Roy Putman was the brother of Frank Putman, the photographer.

78 The staff of Pam's Bakers in High Street, Walton, in 1953. Pam Daniels is on the right.

79 Another Walton High Street shop in the early 1950s – W.J. Bryan, men's outfitters. The shop was eventually taken over by the Clacton firm of Ernest Newson & Son.

80 Stead and Simpson moved into the corner unit of the old Morton Terrace (see plate 25) in the early 1900s and remained there for something like seventy years. This photograph is from the 1950s.

81 The official opening of the new Co-op department store in 1956. It was built next to the old Co-op food store and has now been merged back into it.

82 R. Oxborrow and Sons, blacksmiths of Kirby-le-Soken, earlier this century. The Oxborrow family name had been associated with the forge in Kirby since 1855 and still today an Oxborrow, John, owns the garage which occupies the site.

83 The inside of Ratcliffe's blacksmith shop in Great Holland in the early 1900s.

Ratcliffe's Patent K.I.D. (All British) Lawn Mower.

SUITABLE FOR LARGE OR SMALL LAWNS.

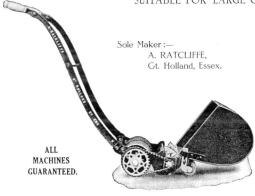

Sole Maker :—
A. RATCLIFFE,
Gt. Holland, Essex.

ALL
MACHINES
GUARANTEED.

¶ This Machine is 12″ Roller drive, fitted with steel chain wheels, the chain drive wheel is fitted with a taper pin; this pin will shear should the Machine come into contact with anything that is likely to damage the blades such as nails, stones, etc. This has often happened and caused expense and annoyance with other Machines. These pins cost only 1 d. and are easy to replace.

¶ The Mower is light and easy to push after several months' wear.

¶ The frame is all one casting and cannot get out of line, will go for a long time without adjustment, even after cutting on rough ground.

¶ The Mower will last a lifetime, at low cost.

¶ All Machines are guaranteed and sent out to any responsible person for one month's free trial, without obligation to purchase.

DESIGNED FOR LONG SERVICE AT LOW COST.

ALL PARTS ARE INTERCHANGEABLE.

THE ABOVE MACHINE FITTED WITH SPECIAL SIDE ROLLERS TO CUT LONG GRASS.

PRICE :

	£	s.	d.
12-in. Machine, complete with Grass Box	4	7	6
Side Rollers for Long Grass		6	0

SOLD BY—

84 Although Ratcliffe's dealt in all fields of iron manufacture, it was for their lawnmowers that they became most famous. This advert from the 1930s explains why!

85 A close-up view of Great Holland's post office and general stores in 1904. The Crampin family ran both businesses from about 1860, when John took them over, until about 1930 when they passed from William's hands to Harold Witney.

86 Fairlight Glen Tea Rooms, Great Holland, in 1906. They were run by Alfred Drinkwater from about the time of this photograph until the 1920s. Alfred Drinkwater was also assistant overseer and clerk to the parish council.

Transport

Commencing Monday, 14th July, 1924.

SPECIAL COAST TRIPS
DAILY
(Sundays included, but Fridays excepted)

by the Magnificent Saloon Steamer

"WALTON BELLE"

Between HARWICH and

FELIXSTOWE, WALTON, CLACTON, SOUTHWOLD, LOWESTOFT AND MARGATE.

SUNDAYS, TUESDAYS AND THURSDAYS.			WEDNESDAYS.		
OUT			**OUT**		
HARWICH (leave)	9.30	a.m.	HARWICH (leave)	8.0	a.m.
FELIXSTOWE ...	10.0	„	CLACTON	9.0	„
WALTON ...	10.30	„	WALTON	9.30	„
CLACTON	11.0	„	FELIXSTOWE ...	10.15	„
MARGATE (arrive)	2.0	p.m.	SOUTHWOLD ...	12.30	p.m.
			LOWESTOFT (arrive)	1.45	„
HOME			**HOME**		
MARGATE (leave)	3.30	„	LOWESTOFT (leave)	3.45	„
CLACTON	6.15	„	SOUTHWOLD ...	4.30	„
WALTON	6.45	„	FELIXSTOWE ...	6 30	„
FELIXSTOWE ...	7.45	„	WALTON	7.10	„
HARWICH (arrive)	8.15	„	CLACTON	7.45	„
			HARWICH (arrive)	8.45	„

Sea Trip from LOWESTOFT from 2 p.m. till 3.30 p.m.
on Wednesdays - 2/-

FARES.
(Including Free Admission to Piers).

Harwich or Felixstowe to—	Single	Return	Clacton to—	Single	Return
			WALTON ...	1/3	2/-
			FELIXSTOWE...	2/-	3/6
WALTON ...	2/-	3/-	SOUTHWOLD...	4/-	6/-
CLACTON ...	2/-	3/6	LOWESTOFT ...	4/6	6/6
MARGATE ...	6/-	10/6	MARGATE ...	4/-	7/-

For Tickets and intermediate Fares, please apply :—

PIER BOOKING OFFICES.

ROYAL SOVEREIGN STEAMSHIP CO., LTD., 7, Swan Lane, London, E.C.4

H. CLARKE & Co. (London) Ltd., 65, Milton St., E.C.2. 52683. 25M. 30 6/24.

87 Practically the only way of getting to Walton in its early days as a seaside resort was by boat. But even after the railway came and the roads had improved, the paddle steamer was still a popular means of travel. The *Walton Belle* was built in 1891 and served the town until 1925 when it was sold to the New Medway Steam Packet Company and renamed *Essex Queen*. It was scrapped in 1932.

Walton-on-the-Naze.

OMNIBUSES

Leave WALTON twice daily (Sundays excepted), at Twenty minutes before Seven in the Morning and Fifteen minutes before Two in the Afternoon, arriving in Colchester for the Parliamentary Train in the Morning, and Forty minutes past Four Quick Train in the Afternoon, returning from the Railway Station, COLCHESTER, on the arrival of the Parliamentary Train at 15 minutes past Ten in the Morning, and on the arrival of the Train at Twenty minutes past Five, which leaves London at Three o'clock in the Afternoon.   An

ADDITIONAL OMNIBUS

On Saturdays, at Eight o'clock, from the Train leaving London at Half-past Five, P.M., returning from Walton on Monday Mornings at Five o'clock, in time for the Market Train to London.

A Cart at the Swan Inn, Colchester, daily for Heavy Goods & Luggage.

Post Horses, Single & Pair-Horse Carriages, on the Shortest Notice.

ROBT. CRESSWELL, Proprietor.

88   Before the railway arrived at Walton in 1867, visitors from London used to catch the train to Colchester and there join one of Robert Cresswell's buses, which would carry them on to the *Marine Hotel.*

89   Frinton also had its own bus service in the early years of this century, as this photograph taken outside the *Grand Hotel* livery stables in 1904 shows. The horse bus used to meet the trains at Frinton station and take the visitors to the sea-front hotels.

90 The area's major bus service between 1913 and 1931 was operated by Clacton & District Motor Services under the fleet name 'Silver Queen'. Unfortunately accidents sometimes happened as on this occasion when the driver, Ted Biggs, drove his bus into a ditch near Great Holland's *Red Lion*!

91 Silver Queen buses were also available for private hire. This 32-seater Leyland Lioness, built in 1927, is pictured here taking a party from the *Red Lion*, Great Holland, on a trip to Suffolk.

92 Coronet Coaches operated from Coronet Service Station (now Frinton Garage) from 1955 to 1962. The one seen here, stuck in the snow and tangled up in fallen telephone wires in Second Avenue on 24 January 1958, had been hired to take schoolchildren from Hawthorn School to Clacton to sit their 11-plus exams. They never made it! Arrangements were made for a re-sit on 14 May.

93 Another local coach company was operated by Charles Barnes from Clacton. He ran it for a while under the fleet name of Progress Coaches. Two of the coaches are seen here posing for a photograph on Pork Lane level crossing in 1933.

94 Frinton station opened on 1 July 1888. A year later the 19-year-old George Cooper, later to be co-founder of Blowers and Cooper, arrived from Diss to become the first clerk at the station. This is the station in 1893. George Cooper is one of the three staff in the photograph, but unfortunately it is not known which one.

95 A class N7 locomotive arrives at Frinton station in 1955. One hundred and thirty four class N7 locomotives were built between 1914 and 1928 and all of them stayed in service until the late 1950s when steam began to disappear from the Frinton and Walton line. The last two to operate on the line were taken from Walton shed on 1 January 1961.

96 The first electric train arrives at Frinton station on 13 April 1959. However, it was not until 1962 that the service to London from Walton, Frinton and Kirby was operated exclusively by electric trains.

97   During the Edwardian period, Frinton had its own volunteer lifeboat. The first was launched in 1901 and was called the *Sailor's Friend*. The second, pictured here, was also called the *Sailor's Friend* and was launched in 1907.

98 Walton also had its volunteer lifeboats but these were in competition with the official R.N.L.I. boats, the first of which, the *Honourable Artillery Company*, was launched in 1884. The R.N.L.I. lifeboat pictured here at its launch in 1954 is the *Edian Courtauld*.

99 The start of a radio revolution: Radio Caroline, housed aboard the M.V. *Mi Amigo*, anchored off Frinton in the mid-1960s. The success of Radio Caroline led to many imitators being set up all round the country and eventually to BBC Radio One.

The Beach and Piers

100   Frinton beach, *c.*1905, with its bathing machines lined up at the water's edge.

101 The west side of Frinton beach. By the 1920s, the bathing machines had given way to the beach huts which lined Frinton's Promenade.

102 The bottom of the Zig Zag on the east side of Frinton beach in the 1920s.

103 Walton's east beach, *c.*1910, with the horse standing by to haul up the bathing machines as the tide comes in. The bathing machines on the east beach were operated by Stephen Carter.

104 Another view of Walton beach from about the same period, this time with a band concert in full swing.

105 Albion Beach, Walton, around the turn of the century, with the camera obscura, one of the first forms of beach entertainment, in evidence. Lined up at the water's edge are more bathing machines, this time operated by Charles Bates; the blocks in the centre were for gentlemen, those either side for ladies.

106 *(above)* Concert parties began to appear on the Albion beach during the Edwardian period. These included Will Pepper's White Coons (with Stanley Holloway and Arthur Askey), Catlin's Pierrots and the Vesta and Victor Concert Party.

107 *(top right)* The Vesta and Victor Concert Party first appeared at Walton in 1904. Their material was criticised in the local press as being of the 'low music hall variety' and for 'throwing ridicule on religion'. They were, however, hugely popular with the crowds who flocked to see their performances.

108 *(bottom right)* Another aspect of Walton's beach just after the end of the First World War, with the new shelters in the background. Still on the beach are a few of Bates's bathing machines and also Hipkin's refreshment kiosk selling ice bricks and Walton rock.

109 Walton's famous huts, which became very popular in the 1920s and '30s, with holidaymakers returning year after year to the same hut.

110 The 1913 sandcastle competition. This has long been a popular amusement on Walton beach. Formerly run by the *Daily Mail*, it is now run under the auspices of the Frinton and Walton Heritage Trust.

The Beach, Walton-on-the-Naze.

111 The beaches at the Naze end, including Hipkin's beach, have never been quite as popular. Nevertheless bathing tents were provided for those who wanted to get away from the bustle of Walton's central beaches.

112 Walton beach, *c.*1950, with the colonnade on the right and in the background the pier with the latest amusements.

113 Walton's first pier was built in 1830. It was built purely as a landing stage for steamers arriving from London and Ipswich, although the charms of its 'agreeable promenade' were also advertised. It was extended several times but was badly damaged in the storm of 1881 and subsequently demolished.

114 Walton's second pier was built by Peter Bruff and opened in the early 1870s. It seems that almost immediately it began to take away the steamer trade from the old pier. This is a very early photograph of the new pier and shows a steamer leaving the pier head.

115   By 1899, the pier was under the control of the Coast Development Company who extended the pier to 2,610 ft., built three berthing arms, a pavilion and ran an electric railway along its length. This photograph was taken *c*.1900 just after the work was completed. The photograph also shows four Belle Steamers at or near the pier head.

116   The entrance to the pier, *c*.1910. Concerts were held in the Pier Pavilion throughout the summer season during the Edwardian era. The Red Incognite Co., from the Royal Agricultural Hall, London, were popular entertainers there.

117 *(above)* In 1927, the date of this photograph, the Sea Spray Lounge on the pier was fitted with 'the latest equipment for perfect services of American ice drinks, sundaes and cream ices'. 'Evocative music' was also played from behind drawn curtains!

118 *(left)* The changing face of Walton pier. This is how the entrance looked in 1970.

DANCING IN PAVILION.

119 *(below)* The original pier railway operated from 1898 until 1935, when it was replaced by a pneumatic-tyred battery car running on wooden beams. During the Second World War the railway was destroyed and was replaced in 1945 by a new 2 ft. gauge miniature railway. This is the pier railway in its final phase in the 1970s.

Sport and Leisure

120   Walton's first summer attraction was the Regatta, which began *c.*1830 and was centred around the old pier. An 1840 guide to Walton describes the Regatta as consisting 'principally in sailing and rowing matches ... concluding with a "duck hunt" ', in which a single man in a small punt was pursued by a large boat.

121   It is said that Frinton owed its development in the late 19th century to the golf club, which was laid out in 1895 by Richard Powell Cooper. The club house was opened in 1899 and moved to its present site in 1903. In 1933 the present Spanish-style entrance and members' lounge were added.

122 By 1904, the golf club had a membership of over three hundred men who played on the full 18-hole course, plus 100 women, who played on a 9-hole course.

123 A young Peter Alliss on the Naze golf course, Walton, with caddie, Mr. Hicks. Plans for this golf course had been made as early as 1908, but were not fulfilled for another 20 years. The course was taken over by the army at the start of the Second World War and was never re-opened.

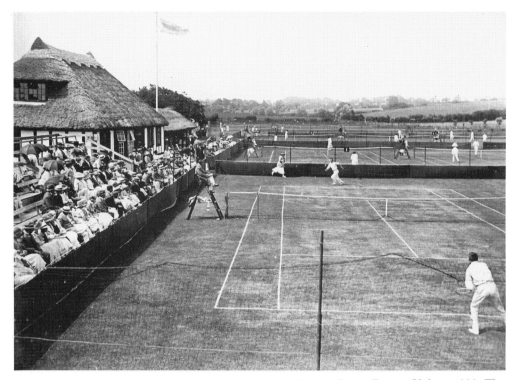

124 Frinton Lawn Tennis Club in 1920. The club was founded in 1900 but reached its height of popularity between the wars, when, under the guidance of its secretary 'Popsy' Bangs, it played host to the cream of British society, including the Prince of Wales, Winston Churchill and film stars such as Gladys Cooper, Gracie Fields and Douglas Fairbanks.

125 Many of the world's top stars played at the annual Frinton tennis tournament, held traditionally the week after Wimbledon. Wimbledon champions who have played in the tournament included Sir Norman Brookes, Kitty McKane, Neal Fraser, Margaret Court and Ann Jones. Pictured above, at the 1933 tournament, is Kay Stammers, a Wimbledon doubles champion and singles finalist.

126   The 1930-1 Walton Town Football Club on their ground at Bath House Meadow. The club had begun in the late 19th century, but in the early years of this century it was disbanded and then reformed in 1922. Its first secretary was Harry Hatcher, on the extreme left in the back row of this picture.

127   In 1939, the club moved to the Frinton Park Estate Ground, where this photograph was taken in 1948-9, the year they won the Tendring Hundred Cup. The club president, Bill Grant, is seventh from the left, back row. When Tendring High School was built on this site, the club moved to its present ground on Frinton Playing Fields.

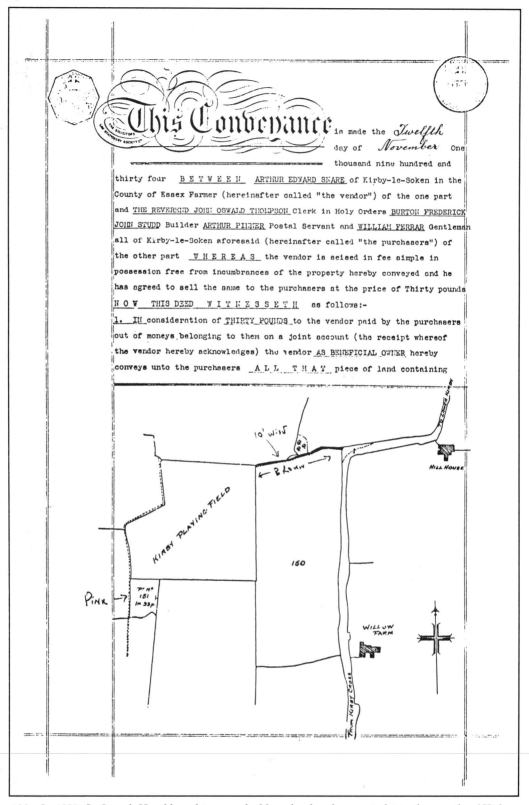

This Conveyance is made the *Twelfth* day of *November* One thousand nine hundred and thirty four B E T W E E N ARTHUR EDWARD SNARE of Kirby-le-Soken in the County of Essex Farmer (hereinafter called "the vendor") of the one part and THE REVEREND JOHN OSWALD THOMPSON Clerk in Holy Orders BURTON FREDERICK JOHN STUDD Builder ARTHUR PILLER Postal Servant and WILLIAM FERRAR Gentleman all of Kirby-le-Soken aforesaid (hereinafter called "the purchasers") of the other part W H E R E A S the vendor is seised in fee simple in possession free from incumbrances of the property hereby conveyed and he has agreed to sell the same to the purchasers at the price of Thirty pounds N O W THIS DEED W I T N E S S E T H as follows:-

1. IN consideration of THIRTY POUNDS to the vendor paid by the purchasers out of moneys belonging to them on a joint account (the receipt whereof the vendor hereby acknowledges) the vendor AS BENEFICIAL OWNER hereby conveys unto the purchasers A L L T H A T piece of land containing

128 In 1927, Sir Joseph Hood bought a parcel of farm land and presented it to the people of Kirby for recreational use. The Kirby Playing Fields Association, consisting of representatives from local sports clubs, was set up to administer it. This is a copy of the conveyance of a second parcel of land, purchased in 1934, and added to the original gift.

129 One of the sports to make full use of the new Kirby Playing Fields was cricket. Kirby Cricket Club was formed in 1928 to begin an association which has lasted to this day. In this photograph, H. Martin and W.D. Harvey go out to bat for Kirby. Wally Harvey was the club captain for 15 years during the 1950s and '60s.

130 Kirby Cricket Club in 1953. In the middle of the back row is Derek Reffell, later Rear-Admiral Derek Reffell. He was appointed Governor of Gibraltar in 1989.

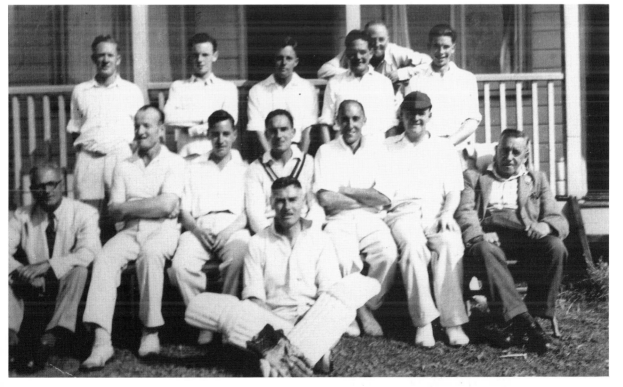

131 Walton Yacht Club in the 1950s. The club house was erected on the site of the old windmill in 1923.

132 A popular amusement in Walton before and after the Second World War was the boating lake set up on the site of the old millpond. In the 1930s it cost one shilling to hire a boat to go all the way round the lake. Children had a choice of rowing boats or paddle boats.

THE BOATING LAKE
WALTON-ON-NAZE

133 Every year on Whit Monday, the five Zion Methodist churches on the Clacton circuit got together to hold a sports day on fields belonging to the Race and Scott Dairy in Kirby Cross. This photograph dates from *c.*1912.

134 Popular events at the Zion Methodist Whit Monday meeting included running races, novelty races such as the egg and spoon and the threading the needle race, tug-of-war, brass bands and the event pictured here in 1911, the ladies' football match. The Whit Monday meeting came to an end in 1932 when the Zionists merged with the Wesleyans.

135 Tobogganing in Frinton, 1909. When the snow came, home-made amusements were the order of the day. In the background is Frinton Boys' College in Second Avenue. Founded in 1907, it advertised its 'lofty and well-ventilated rooms' and prepared boys for 'public school and the Royal Navy'.

136 Frinton's Lido, situated on the cliff top where the Leas car park now is, was built in the early 1920s. It consisted of a dance hall and a cafe and also boasted an 18-hole miniature golf course. It was meant to be the leisure centre for the new Frinton Park Estate, but worries about erosion finally killed it off and it was demolished in 1936.

137 Walton has had two cinemas. The first, the Kino, seen here in the 1920s, was situated on Princes Esplanade. During the Second World War it was commandeered by the army and used for lectures. It closed not long after the war and became first a café and later an amusement arcade.

138 The second cinema was the Regal, opened in 1934 and photographed here in the early 1950s with a group of children from the infant school led by their teacher, Miss Cole. The Regal closed in the late 1960s; it was replaced in Walton High Street by Woolworth's.

139 The Walton Carnival, a popular annual event. This view dates from 1956 and shows the sea cadet band leading the procession.

140 The Frinton Darby and Joan Club taking part in the 1955 Walton Carnival in one of Mr. F.G. Pollendine's Coronet Coaches decorated as 'The Good Old Days'. For this special occasion the driver was Mr. Pollendine himself, while the company's usual driver, Jack Entiknapp, sat on top. Also sitting on top were Mrs. R. Crampin and Mrs. Betty Gardner.

Events

141 The 1907 launch of the Frinton voluntary lifeboat, the *Sailor's Friend*.

142 Frinton's fire brigade put on an annual display of fire-fighting techniques on the greensward both before and after the First World War. This is the 1908 display in progress.

143 Trees were planted in both Kirby Cross and Kirby-le-Soken to celebrate King George V's coronation in 1911. The Kirby Cross tree was on the triangle at the corner of Frinton Road and Halstead Road.

CORONATION TREE PLANTING, KIRBY CROSS.

144 This photograph of Frinton Lawn Tennis Club was taken by 'Popsy' Bangs' daughter, Betty, on the morning of 8 July 1927 after a torrential downpour. Courts were flooded to net height and the Frinton Tournament, due to take place the following week, was cancelled.

145 The Duke of Kent officially opens Princes Esplanade, Walton, 30 July 1930 and, although it has already been in service for two years, officially launches the new Walton lifeboat, the *E.M.E.D.* On the left, watching, is Mr. William Oxley, secretary of the lifeboat.

146 The dedication of the new lych-gate at All Saints Church, Great Holland, *c.*1935.

147 The 1936 Mummery and Harris fire at its height. By the time it was over, the shop in Connaught Avenue was completely destroyed. The inset in the top left shows the shop, which had been built only one year earlier, before the conflagration. The rebuilt shop can be seen on the right in the next plate.

148 Frinton's Connaught Avenue, decked out for the 1937 Coronation celebrations. The main event of the day was the 'Olde English Village Fayre' held on 'ye Great Fielde on ye North side of ye road from Frinton to Walton'. The celebration included Pongo the Clown and a tug-of-war competition between Frinton, Walton, Kirby and Great Holland.

149 The east coast floods which took place on the night of 31 January/ 1 February 1953 brought chaos to the Essex coast, with places like Jaywick and Canvey Island suffering much loss of life. Although no actual lives were lost in Frinton or Walton they both felt the full force of the severe weather that night occasioning untold damage to property.

150 1953 also saw the coronation of Queen Elizabeth II, and the four parishes once again came together to celebrate. This is the float entered by Coronation Garage in the carnival procession being made ready outside Kirby Cross station. It won second prize in the decorated float category.

151 A British legion rally on Walton beach, 12 September 1954.

People

152   Sterndale School, Harold Way, Frinton, *c.*1938. Sterndale started life just before the First World War in Walton Lodge. It transferred to no. 4 Ashlyn's Road, Frinton, at the beginning of the war and then moved to Harold Way, *c.*1926.

153 Walton Primary School's football team in the 1920s on Bath House Meadow.

154 The domestic science class at Walton School, 1946. The headmaster, Mr. Landsdowne, is second from the left.

155   Kirby Primary School, shortly after it was opened in 1901. The headmaster at this time was John William Balm.

156   At the beginning of the Second World War, Great Holland School was commandeered by the army. Those children not evacuated attended classes in various houses around the village. This group photograph was taken by the teacher, Miss Gronjon, outside her own house in Pork Lane during the winter of 1940-1.

photo.
ELLIS.
MALTA

157 The Duke of Connaught. It was in his honour that Station Road, Frinton, was renamed Connaught Avenue on 17 September 1904 at a ceremony performed by his wife. He had been staying at the *Grand Hotel* earlier that week while umpiring military manoeuvres in the area.

158 A group of workers from F. Dennett, a building firm from Peckham, London, take time off from building the *Esplanade Hotel*, Frinton, to have their photograph taken. The date is 21 March 1902.

159 Mr. Rowlands, Frinton's first permanent live-in level crossing gate-keeper from 1896-1921 and father of James Walker Rowlands, owner of Rowlands Ironmonger's in Old Road.

160 Frinton's Fire Brigade give colleague Charlie Moon and his bride a big send-off on their wedding day, 4 April 1934. The Dennis fire engine was Frinton's first motorised fire engine.

161 The annual dinner laid on by Frinton Urban District Council for the fire brigade took place at the *Queen's Hotel* in 1938. Captain Roberts is fourth from the left, back row. Other well-known firemen include Charlie Moon, seated second from the end on the right-hand side and Ernie Pink, at the top of the second row from the right.

162 The Frinton Fire Brigade line up outside the Service Garage in Connaught Avenue in 1939, having just had a hundred per cent success rate in their gas mask exams.

163 Jonas Oxley, well-known cox of Walton lifeboat from 1947 to 1964, pictured here in 1954. He was awarded a bronze medal for gallantry in 1939 whilst second cox and a second service clasp in 1964. He was also a fine painter of British birds.

164 Frank Putman, founder of Putman's Photographic Studio, in 1953. Putman started his business in 1921 in his garden shed. He later moved to a proper studio in Walton High Street and in 1971 sold the business to David West and Peter Frost. Mrs. Jessie Putman, who carried on the business during the Second World War, when Frank joined the RAF, is on the left.

165 Walton councillor Alf South during his year of office as chairman of the council, 1953-4. As vice-chairman the previous year he had played a prominent part in helping the flood victims of the east coast floods. He owned a dairy in Old Pier Street.

166 Well-known local personality, Susannah Hatcher, seen returning to her home in Walton from London where she had been to witness at first hand the coronation celebrations of 1953. She was a keen supporter of Walton Town football club.

167 The Great Holland Institute Brass Band, *c.*1910. The drummer is Mr. Charles Parmenter.

168   Second from the right, swinging on the gate of the family house on the main Clacton Road, Great Holland, around the turn of the century, is a young Elsie Derrett. Elsie later married Archie Ratcliffe (see plate 74).

169 Ratcliffe's foundry was turned over to making munitions during the Second World War. Here a group of workers outside the factory show off their wares.

170 Harry Crampin, from Great Holland's well-known Crampin family, gives Fred Morris, a member of another old Great Holland family, a tow near the *Red Lion*, *c*.1920.

171   A photograph taken *c.*1905 of Great Holland's heroes. All had served with the army. Seated second from the left is Charles Crampin, believed to be the only man ever to be awarded two Distinguished Conduct Medals, at Burma in 1899 and South Africa in 1900. Herbert Digby, seated far right, served at Omdurman.

Bibliography

Allen, C.J., *The Great Eastern Railway* (1955)

Bloom, U., *Rosemary for Frinton* (1970)

Box, P., *Belles of the East Coast* (1989)

Boyden, P.B. and Bates, P.F., *The Growth of Frinton, 1600-1914* (1973)

Boyden, P.B., *Frinton before the Stuarts* (1978)

Boyden, P.B., *The First 124,999,061 Years of Walton* (1979)

Boyden, P.B., *The Resort that became a Town* (1995)

Boyden, P.B., *Three Studies in Victorian Walton* (1987)

Boyden, P.B., *Walton, 1800-1867* (1981)

Hicks, T.W. and Smith, D.H.A., *The Story of the Churches of Frinton* (1952)

Jacobs, N., *The Sunshine Coast* (1986)

Johnson, I., *Turning Point* (1982)

Lilley, J. and Oxborrow, R., *A Walk through the Streets of Kirby Past* (1993)

Markham, R., *Geologists' Association Guide to the Estuarine Region of Suffolk and Essex: Walton-on-the-Naze and Wrabness* (1973)

Modlen, L.C., *The Story of Walton-le-Soken* (*c.*1955)

Norman, B.J., *Walton-on-the-Naze in Old Picture Postcards* (1983)

Paine, D., *The History and Work of the Walton and Frinton Lifeboat* (*c.*1984)

Palmer, K., *Setting the Record Straight!!* (1994)

Palmer, K., *Wish You Were Here* (1992)

Peart, S., *The Picture House in East Anglia* (1980)

Pertwee, N., *Frinton-on-Sea Lawn Tennis Club* (1975)

Phillips, C., *The Tendring Hundred Railway* (1989)

Pratt, R., *Aeduluesnasa: Kirby in History* (*c.*1992)

Rouse, M., *Coastal Resorts of East Anglia* (1982)

Russell, J.M., *100 Years of Frinton's Railway* (1989)

Warner, H.F., *Walton-on-the-Naze Yesterday and Today* (1993)